OXFORDSHIRE BUSES

JOHN LAW

AMBERLEY

Front cover top: South Midland Bristol VR/ECW 615 at Gloucester Green, Oxford, in December 1986.

Front cover bottom: Heyfordian NAL 544F, an ex West Bridgeford UDC AEC Swift/East Lancs bus, seen at the depot in 1977.

Back cover: Oxford South Midland Daimler Fleetline/Alexander 411 at Gloucester Green bus station, Oxford, on a wet day in the mid-1970s.

First published 2015

Amberley Publishing
The Hill, Stroud
Gloucestershire, GL5 4EP

www.amberley-books.com

British Library Cataloguing in Publication Data.
A catalogue record for this book is available from the British Library.

ISBN 978 1 4456 4672 5 (print)
ISBN 978 1 4456 4673 2 (ebook)

Typeset in 10pt on 13pt Sabon.
Typesetting and Origination by Amberley Publishing.
Printed in the UK.

Introduction

Oxfordshire could be described as a county of contrasts. The county's only city, Oxford, well known for its universities, is a bustling place, busy with students, tourists and shoppers. However, it is not a big place, being around the same size as many medium-sized towns in the United Kingdom. In comparison, the other towns of Oxfordshire, for example Chipping Norton, Abingdon or Wantage, are small market towns. Only Banbury, in north Oxfordshire, could possibly be called a major town.

South of Oxford, we are in commuter country, the Thames Valley serving as dormitory land for London, Reading and Oxford itself. North Oxfordshire, once beyond the boundaries of Oxford itself, is very rural. The extreme north and west of the county, having boundaries with Gloucestershire, Warwickshire and Northamptonshire, are often regarded as part of the South Midlands.

I first visited Oxfordshire in 1973, finding that the city of Oxford was a fascinating place for a bus enthusiast like myself. The main operator here carried the fleetname Oxford South Midland, though the legal lettering always showed City of Oxford Motor Services. At the time, the company owned a mainly AEC bus fleet, though other marques were also to be seen on the county's roads and streets. One type of bus rarely seen in Oxfordshire was the Leyland National. Oxford South Midland never ordered any and only one example appears in these pages.

Oxford South Midland was a National Bus Company subsidiary, formed in 1971 by combining the resources of City of Oxford Motor Services (COMS) and South Midland. The latter had been the coaching arm of Thames Valley, while COMS could trace its history back to the days of horse trams in the city. In 1969, the National Bus Company had absorbed both companies.

Gradually, corporate NBC red livery was applied, until Margaret Thatcher came along and decided to privatise the bus industry. In preparation, in 1983, Oxfordshire's main bus company was split up, with the Oxford Bus Company running mostly city services and a new South Midland concern having the more rural routes. 1986 saw deregulation introduced, allowing competition between the two. Nowhere was this more felt than on the London routes via the M40 motorway, where the two main operators compete to this day.

Privatisation eventually saw the Oxford Bus Company sold to the Go Ahead Group, still the case at the time of writing.

South Midland was bought out by its management, later becoming Thames Transit, under which name it was purchased by Harry Blundred of Devon General fame, bringing a host of minibuses to Oxford's streets. The entire Devon General empire was soon sold to the Stagecoach Group.

In the north of the county, around Banbury, Midland Red was originally the dominant bus company. The pre-privatisation split saw the operations there become part of Midland Red South, nowadays another part of Stagecoach.

Other major operators were also to be seen in Oxfordshire, including Bristol Omnibus Company, running in from Swindon, while Alder Valley ran services in and around Henley-on-Thames. The Berkshire and Oxfordshire operations of Alder Valley later became known as Bee Line. In 1990, the Oxford Bus Company purchased the High Wycombe operations of Bee Line, but ten years later sold them on to Arriva, including the Oxford to Aylesbury service, bringing yet another livery to Oxford.

In addition to the big boys, there have been, indeed there still are, many smaller independent bus and coach operators. Banbury, for example, saw Geoff Amos Coaches (from Northamptonshire), Tanners Coaches, Heyfordian and others. The city of Oxford was also a destination for many independents. My favourite was always Charlton-on-Otmoor Services, with a fleet of smartly turned out AEC buses and coaches. The company still survives, but nowadays has no AECs or stage carriage operations into the city.

Many smaller companies have fallen by the wayside. Motts (Yellow Buses) and Chiltern Queens, for example, are fondly remembered. A fairly recent casualty was RH Transport, which operated several services around Oxford. Thames Travel was a relative newcomer to the south Oxfordshire bus scene, but was taken over by the Go Ahead Group in 2011, albeit kept as a separate concern.

The stories of all these bus operators are told within these pages, mainly in pictures taken by myself, supplemented by several from Richard Huggins, who got to a few of the more minor depots in the 1970s and 1980s. I must also acknowledge the Internet site 'Bus Lists on the Web', which has saved me hours of trawling through various publications during the research for this book.

Arriving at Oxford railway station in 1973, the first Oxford South Midland bus to be seen was fleet number 63 (419 DHO), an AEC Reliance with Park Royal dual-purpose coachwork. This vehicle was new in 1962 to Aldershot & District and was one of several transferred into Oxford from the South Midland fleet.

Alongside 63 (above) was number 338 (338 RJO), one of many AEC Renowns remaining in the Oxford South Midland fleet. It is seen still bearing pre-National Bus Company livery, albeit with NBC corporate logos on its sides. Carrying Park Royal bodywork, this AEC Renown, built in 1963, was one of the last of the AEC double-deckers built for City of Oxford. Previously, COMS had received AEC Regents (both Mark III and V) and AEC Bridgemasters, though all had been taken out of service by the time of my first visit.

In 1973, Oxford's main bus station was an open air affair at Gloucester Green, with Oxford South Midland and other major operators using the main stands and parking areas, while independent buses and other companies were relegated to a stand on one side, with no passenger facilities. Not that other voyagers were afforded much comfort in other parts of the bus station either! One of the last AEC Reliances, number 52 (SWL 52J), with dual-purpose Willowbrook forty-nine-seat coachwork, is receiving some attention in the parking area. Attending the problem is the company's fine Leyland towing vehicle.

Another 1972 AEC Reliance/Willowbrook semi-coach, number 49 (SWL 49J) is seen in Oxford city centre. Unlike the previous photo, this vehicle is carrying the National Bus Company's red and white dual-purpose colours. In 1973, it is captured on film negotiating Cornmarket Street while heading for London via High Wycombe. This thoroughfare has since been pedestrianised.

After it became impossible to order new AEC double-deckers, City of Oxford turned to Daimler Fleetlines to fulfil their requirements. Here is a typical example, delivered in 1971, still in pre-NBC colours in Cornmarket Street, Oxford, in 1973. Number 414 (TFC 414K) has Alexander bodywork and is heading for Aylesbury via Thame.

Northern Counties of Wigan also supplied bodies for City of Oxford's Daimler Fleetlines. One of these, number 424 (UFC 424K), was photographed in 1973, again in Cornmarket Street, Oxford. Prominent in the background is St Michael in the Northgate church, with its Saxon tower dating back to the year 1040.

A non-standard double-decker in the Oxford South Midland fleet was number 204 (UBX 48), a 1959-built Leyland Atlantean PDR1/1 with lowbridge Weymann bodywork. This had been purchased by City of Oxford in 1971, but was new to south Wales independent James of Ammanford. It was later sold to Derby City Transport for further service and has since been preserved. I found it in Oxford city centre, operating a local service in 1973.

Having seen much in the city centre, I took a trip out to Oxford South Midland's main depot on Cowley Road, Oxford. Nicely posed in the depot was fleet number 22 (LJB 422E), a Bristol RELH6G/ECW forty-seven-seat semi-coach. This had been inherited from Thames Valley's South Midland business. The original Oxford South Midland fleetname is clearly shown here, but it was soon to disappear in favour of the National Bus Company's double-arrow logo.

Another former Thames Valley coach in Oxford South Midland's livery is seen here pressed into a stage carriage service due to a vehicle shortage. It is quite a rare coach for a big company, being a Harrington Crusader-bodied Bedford SB3, registered EMO 551C. The coach was originally intended for the London service. It carried fleet number 10 when seen on Cowley Road, Oxford, in 1973.

The aforementioned bus shortage meant that several former Thames Valley coaches were being used on local bus services during my visit in 1973. Bristol MW5G/ECW number 42 (618 JPU) was new in 1957 to Eastern National. I found it in Oxford city centre, again in 1973.

The 1973 crisis in the Oxford South Midland fleet meant that several buses and coaches were hired in from various operators. One that had travelled well away from home was Barton of Nottinghamshire number 776 (YNN 776). This 1958 AEC Reliance/Alexander C37F coach was found in Gloucester Green bus station, about to go onto a stand and take up service. The snack bar seen in the background was by far the best in Gloucester Green, as I found that both the offerings and the clientele in the official bus station café left a lot to be desired.

Midland Red also supplied some buses to help out in Oxford in 1973. Built by Midland Red themselves was this S16 single decker, number 5126 (5126 HA), in its parent fleet. It is seen on a local service negotiating pedestrianised Queen Street and approaching the Carfax Tower.

Swindon Corporation 138 (SMR 138B), a 1964 AEC Reliance with a dual-doored Willowbrook body, is seen on loan to Oxford South Midland in 1973. Photographed in Cornmarket Street, Oxford, it is about to be overtaken by Daimler Fleetline 423.

Moving forward in time now to about 1975, here's Oxford South Midland 353 (CFC 353C) posed nicely in Gloucester Green, Oxford, with some lightweight Willowbrook saloons adding a bit of modernity to the scene. 353 is a standard AEC Renown/Park Royal vehicle.

Most of Oxford's AEC Renowns wore Park Royal bodywork, but here is an exception. Number 368 (FWL 368E), delivered in summer 1967, is an example of the products of Northern Counties, capable of carrying sixty-five seated passengers. Again, we're at Gloucester Green, Oxford, this time around 1974.

In the 1970s, City of Oxford turned to Bristol to supply single-deck buses and coaches. New in 1972 was number 72 (GBW 72L), a Bristol RELH6G with ECW forty-nine-seat coach bodywork. It is seen in Gloucester Green bus station, Oxford, prior to receiving National Bus Company livery. The minimal waiting facilities for the public are obvious in this photo, taken around 1975.

A visit to Oxfordshire on 6 June 1974 saw me take a ride out to Oxford South Midland's Cowley Road depot. Here is a peek inside, showing two AEC Renowns, a pair of AEC Reliance saloons and a couple of Bedford/Harrington coaches. The latter look rather sorry for themselves and had probably been withdrawn from service.

Seen sometime around 1976 on an Aylesbury run in central Oxford is fleet number 906 (NAC 417F). Unusually for Oxford South Midland, it is a Leyland Atlantean PDRA/1 with bodywork by Northern Counties. It was new to Stratford Blue as number 11 in 1967.

On 22 April 1974, I ventured into the more rural parts of Oxfordshire. Arriving at Didcot station on a Chiltern Queens AEC Reliance, I transferred to Oxford South Midland's 60 (VNT 848J). The two buses are seen here posing for the camera with GWR architecture as a backdrop. Number 60 was new to a Shropshire operator, Coopers of Oakengates, which had recently succumbed to the might of Midland Red. Though in full Oxford South Midland colours, Midland Red retained ownership of this 1971 Bedford YRQ/Willowbrook forty-five-seater.

On arrival at Wantage aboard vehicle number 60, I could not resist this picture of the dual-purpose, liveried, lightweight bus posed outside the small depot. A reminder of the old order is plainly visible over the depot doors.

On the same day as the previous two pictures, I was granted permission to freely roam around the Wantage depot of Oxford South Midland and take photographs. Several buses were still in the old pre-NBC colours, such as this 1962 AEC Reliance/Marshall fifty-three-seat bus, number 771 (771 NJO), seen in the confines of the depot building. The bus later saw service with Scottish independent Irvine's of Law.

Many Oxford South Midland buses based at Wantage were stored outside. Here is a pair of Park Royal bodied AEC Renowns, a marque that could be regarded as the standard double-deck bus of the former City of Oxford fleet until the early 1970s. Closest to my camera is number 351 (CFC 351C), bearing NBC red livery, while a sister vehicle behind it still carries the previous colour scheme. In the left background, the yard of Regis Coaches can be seen. We will pay a visit here further within these pages.

Another occupant of Wantage depot yard on 22 April 1974 was this small 1963-built AEC Reliance/Marshall forty-four-seater, number 778 (778 PJO). Like many of its type, it never received NBC red livery and was scrapped soon after I saw it.

I returned to rural Oxfordshire on 6 June 1974, when I photographed another Marshall-bodied AEC Reliance (though delivered in 1961) during a crew change in Wallingford. Number 760 (760 MFC) carries pre-NBC colours, contrasting nicely with the Town Hall behind.

Sometime around 1975, Daimler Fleetline/Alexander 404 (TFC 404K) is seen in Gloucester Green, Oxford, having a clean-up prior to working a schools service. Like many of Oxford South Midland's double-deck fleet, this bus is to dual-door configuration.

Not all Oxford's 'deckers were dual-doored. Here is single-door Bristol VRT/SL6G with ECW H43/34F bodywork, number 433 (OUD 433M), new in 1974. It is seen in central Oxford when it was about a year old, passing a fine Southern Gas Austin van and Oxford's oldest building, St Michael at the Northgate church.

Now we are back in Oxford's Gloucester Green bus station, sometime around 1975. In the foreground is Oxford South Midland 74 (XBW 74M), a Bristol RELH/Plaxton forty-seat coach, bearing NBC dual-purpose livery. This vehicle was later transferred to Hampshire Bus and subsequently sold to Isle Coaches of Owston Ferry, north Lincolnshire. It was scrapped in 1989. Oxford South Midland's offices can be seen in the background. This building was once the Central Boys School. It later became a pub, then a restaurant.

This 1971 AEC Reliance with Willowbrook coachwork is a typical saloon of the Oxford South Midland fleet in the 1970s. Originally a dual-purpose vehicle, 751 (SWL 51J) is seen in NBC red bus livery at Gloucester Green, Oxford, in 1977.

Against a backdrop of Gloucester Green's bus station café in central Oxford is Oxford South Midland's fleet number 39 (YBL 928H). This Bristol LH6L/Duple Viceroy forty-one-seat coach was inherited from Thames Valley's South Midland operation, in whose fleet it was number 439.

The 1970s saw the National Bus Company ordering lightweight single-deck buses. 1976 saw the delivery of fifty Ford R1014/Duple Dominant saloons to various NBC subsidiaries. Eight of these went to Oxford South Midland and an example, number 666 (WWL503R), is seen at Gloucester Green, Oxford, in 1977.

Earlier lightweight buses included a batch of Ford R1014 1973-built chassis. All were bodied by Willowbrook, with forty-five seats. Here is number 658 (NWL 658M) in the yard of Witney depot, basking in the sun on 27 August 1978. Thanks to Richard Huggins for allowing use of this photo.

Also photographed by Richard Huggins at Witney depot on 27 August 1978 was coach-seated Bristol VRTSL6G/ECW number 106 (NUD 106L). Painted in NBC dual-purpose livery, vehicles like this were intended to be used on the longer distance inter-urban routes.

The deficiencies of the waiting facilities at Gloucester Green bus station, Oxford, are clearly seen in this photo. Luckily, it had just stopped raining! Dual-purpose-liveried Bristol VRTSL6G/ECW number 107 (NUD 107L) is awaiting its next working on a Bicester service in 1977.

On 27 August 1978, my friend Richard Huggins visited Oxford South Midland's Wantage garage, where he found a pair of ECW-bodied Bristol VRTSL6G 'deckers. Nearest the camera is 438 (GUD 750N), while behind is 442 (JWL 995N). Both are to a single-doorway configuration, unlike many of the company's Bristol VRs used on Oxford city services.

Bristol VRTSL6G/ECW H43/34F number 451 (TBW 451P) posed nicely outside Witney depot on 27 August 1978. Photograph by Richard Huggins.

Richard Huggins, during his tour of Oxfordshire's depots on 27 August 1978, also visited Faringdon outstation. Here he found Oxford South Midland number 54 (TJO 54K), a 1971-built AEC Reliance with Marshall dual-purpose coachwork, bearing the appropriate NBC livery of the time.

A pair of unusual vehicles in the Oxford South Midland fleet is seen here at Gloucester Green, Oxford, in 1977. Numbers 26 (CRN 833D) and 28 (CRN 835D) are both Plaxton Panorama-bodied, 1966-built Leyland Leopards. Both were new to Ribble Motor Services, in whose fleet they were fleet numbers 833 and 835 respectively.

Staying at Gloucester Green, but in early 1980, we find Oxford South Midland number 376 (KFC 376G). This is a 1968-built Daimler Fleetline CRG6LX with Wigan-built Northern Counties single-door bodywork.

A portent of things to come in the mid-1980s! Oxford South Midland 705 (VYM 502M) is a Ford Transit minibus. New in 1974 to National Travel (South-East), this Strachans fifteen-seat van conversion was soon transferred to Oxfordshire. It is seen at Gloucester Green around 1976. It was later sold to South Wales Transport. This was only one of three in the fleet at the time, but plenty more Ford Transits were soon to arrive and are still to come within these pages.

Ready for a trip to Chipping Norton in 1981 is Oxford South Midland 439 (GUD 751N), seen at Gloucester Green, Oxford. The bus is a standard Bristol VRTSL6G of late 1974 vintage. It has single-door ECW seventy-seven-seat coachwork. It later saw service with Devon General and Scottish independent Moffat & Williamson.

Oxford South Midland was one of only a few National Bus Company businesses that ordered dual-doored Bristol VR double-deckers. Number 484 (OUD 484T), delivered in November 1978, is a VRT/SL3/6LXB with a ECW H43/27D body. This bus was later exported to Charleroi, in Belgium, after further PSV service with Luton & District. Behind 484, seen in Gloucester Green, Oxford, is Ind Coope's Greyhound pub, one of two watering holes serving the bus station. The other was Morrell's Welsh Pony. Both pubs have since closed.

Seen when almost new at Gloucester Green in 1979 is Oxford South Midland number 14 (RFC 14T), a Duple Dominant coach-bodied Leyland Leopard, resplendent in NBC dual-purpose red and white livery. It was later given a Willowbrook Warrior body and saw further service with various other operators, including services in Bournemouth and Brighton.

The late 1970s saw the introduction of park and ride services in Oxford. A small fleet of ex-London Transport DMS type Daimler Fleetlines was purchased by Oxford South Midland to assist in the operation of this new service. The DMS was a type of bus that had been introduced to London in the 1970s, but soon fell out of favour with LT, becoming a source of quickly available second-hand buses. Number 994 (JGU 275K), with Metro-Cammell bodywork, is seen in central Oxford in dedicated Park and Ride colours in early 1980. It had previously been DMS 1275 in the London fleet.

Another ex-London Transport DMS in the Oxford South Midland fleet is seen here in Magdalen Street, Oxford, 1980. Number 998 (MLH 371L), ex-DMS 1371, bears standard NBC poppy-red livery. It is being used on a local service, as is the Bristol VR behind.

The express services from Oxfordshire to London can certainly be regarded as a great success, right up to the present day. These have been able to compete with the rail service by being able to go direct to London via the M40, while trains have to travel via Didcot and Reading. In addition, coaches can penetrate central London, whereas the railway terminates at Paddington, thereby involving a Tube or local bus journey to get to one's destination. Most of the smaller Oxfordshire towns have no rail service, an example being Wantage. It is here that we see Oxford South Midland number 6 (LWL 6S), painted in NBC dual-purpose livery. This 1978-built Leyland Leopard/Duple Dominant coach is operating route 390 to London.

Oxford South Midland's London routes terminated at Victoria in the capital. Having just left the coach station at that location, number 27 (MUD 27W) is seen starting out on its journey to Carterton via Oxford and Witney when almost new. This 1981-built Leyland Leopard/Duple Dominant coach was to receive a Willowbrook Warrior bus body in 1990 and had a good long life in that guise.

The special Oxford to London livery employed on dedicated coaches operating that service is seen to good advantage on Oxford South Midland 32 (VUD 32X). This 1982 Leyland Leopard/Eastern Coach Works forty-nine-seat coach was found in Victoria Coach Station in the year of its delivery.

A more unusual Oxford South Midland coach to bear the 'City Link' livery was number 47 (KET 161W). This 1981-built Leyland Leopard/Willowbrook coach was new to Yorkshire Traction, but was soon transferred to Oxfordshire. It is seen in London's Victoria Coach Station in 1982. This type of bodywork was quite common within NBC subsidiaries, but quickly fell out of favour.

An earlier coach employed on the London service is seen here at Gloucester Green, Oxford, in 1982. Number 72 (GBW 72L) is a Bristol RELH6G/ECW forty-nine-seat coach, new in 1972 and photographed in NBC dual-purpose colours. Luckily, it is a dry day, though the waiting passengers do not appear to approve of the minimal facilities.

Another Bristol/ECW combination was found at Gloucester Green some time in 1981. Number 678 (JEH 178K) is a Bristol RELL6L, new to Potteries Motor Traction in 1972. Originally dual-doored, it was later converted to single door, as seen here in Oxford South Midland's ownership.

On 12 September 1981, my friend Richard Huggins attended an open day at Oxford South Midland's main Oxford depot, on Cowley Road. Here he found this dual-doored 1978 Bristol VRT/SL3/6LXB with ECW bodywork, number 476 (HUD 476S), resplendent in the old City of Oxford colours. It had been painted in this livery to celebrate 100 years of the company. The vehicle has since been preserved and resides in the Oxford Bus Museum at Long Hanborough.

The Oxford Bus Museum is home to several former City of Oxford buses and it is appropriate that a couple of examples of the collection are shown within these pages. Looking very smart within the confines of the museum building is this 1957-built AEC Regent V/Park Royal, number 956 (956 AJO). It was photographed in June 1998.

The premises of the Oxford Bus Museum are situated next to Hanborough railway station, still open to passengers, on the Oxford to Worcester line. Alternatively, it is only a few miles from Blenheim Palace and the small town of Witney, so is easy to get to. During a visit in June 1998, City of Oxford AEC Regal III/Willowbrook thirty-two-seater number 727 (OJO 727) was found in the yard. After withdrawal from Oxfordshire, this bus went to Burnett's of Mintlaw, near Aberdeen, for further service. Burnett's were later taken over by Alexander (Northern) and OJO 727 received that company's yellow livery. It was withdrawn in September 1972 and is now back in home territory, in its original colours.

As mentioned in the introduction, in 1983 Oxford South Midland was split into two companies, South Midland and Oxford Bus Company. The latter retained NBC poppy-red livery for some years, but then introduced a new colour scheme. It is seen here applied to dual-door Bristol VRT/SL3/6LXB number 478 (HUD 478S), seen beside Oxford railway station on an unrecorded date. This bus was new to Oxford South Midland in 1978.

The mid-1980s saw the modernisation of the Oxford Bus Company's coach fleet. One foul day in January 1985, I found number 115 (A115 PBW) at Gloucester Green, Oxford. This fifty-seat Leyland Tiger/Plaxton 'Paramount 3500 Express' coach has City Link livery for the London services.

Similar vehicle 113 (A113 MUD), a 1984-built Leyland Tiger, has a standard Plaxton Paramount body. Again, it is seen at Gloucester Green, Oxford, in January 1985, ready for a quick trip via the motorway to London on route 190.

NBC red livery, with 'Oxford' fleetnames, is carried by Oxford Bus Company number 986 (MPT 316P), seen in central Oxford in December 1986. This 1975 Leyland Atlantean AN68/1R, with ECW H45/27D bodywork, was transferred from Northern General.

The mid-1980s saw Oxford experience a boom in minibus services. The Oxford Bus Company owned a fleet of Ford Transits, advertising themselves as 'Oxford City Nipper' and using this dedicated livery. Number 728 (C728 JJO) is seen outside the Debenham's store in Magdalen Street in December 1986. New in July of that year, 728 carries a Carlyle twenty-seat body.

Oxford's park and ride services expanded considerably during the 1980s and were well established by late 1989, when I photographed Oxford Bus Company number 229 (E229 CFC) heading south out of the city centre. This 1988-built Leyland Olympian has dual-doored Alexander bodywork.

Also on park and ride duties in central Oxford was number 613 (RFC 13T), seen in the summer of 1991. This unusual bus was one of several Oxford Bus Company vehicles that had received replacement Willowbrook Warrior bus bodies. It had been new to Oxford South Midland in 1978 as a Leyland Leopard with a forty-nine-seat Duple Dominant coach body.

It is a sunny day early in 1993 and Oxford Bus Company number 239 (FWL 781Y) is loading up in the centre of the city. According to my records, this 1983-built Leyland Olympian/ECW was originally a dual-doored bus, but is seen here with a single door and in the latest colour scheme of the day.

In the 1990s, Oxford Bus Company purchased a batch of Optare Metroriders to replace the Ford Transits. Number 770 (G770 WFC) is a twenty-three-seat example, in 'Oxford City Nipper' livery, seen entering the city centre in early 1993.

Like many provincial operators at the time, Oxford Bus Company purchased a small batch of former London Buses Leyland Titans. Number 963 (OHV 727Y) is an example, having been new to London Transport in 1983 as fleet number T727. It is seen outside Oxford railway station in mid-1994.

By the 1990s, Oxford's Gloucester Green had been drastically changed. Part had become a square, with shops and cafés. The new coach station occupied the other half, which was much smaller than the previous incarnation. However, the passenger facilities were much improved. In this mid-1994 photograph, the old information office (formerly Central Boys School) can be seen in the left background. The main subject of the photo is Oxford Bus Company 150 (L150 HUD), a Volvo B10M-62 coach with Plaxton bodywork, departing for Heathrow.

An interesting development in the 1990s was the introduction of the 'City Circuit' by Oxford Bus Company. With input from Oxfordshire County Council and Southern Electric, a battery-operated eighteen-seat Optare Metrorider was used to transport travellers around the city centre. Here is number 803 (L803 HJO) at the charging point outside Oxford railway station in mid-1994. This pioneering venture sadly only lasted four years. I am grateful to the *Oxford Mail* for much of the above information.

The Mitre Inn, on Oxford's high street, was built in the seventeenth century, but can trace its history back even further. Passing the hostelry in mid-1996 is Oxford Bus Company 511 (M511 VJO), a Dennis Dart/Marshall saloon built in 1995. The Dennis Dart was very popular with many operators during the decade.

This Oxford Bus Company Volvo B10B/Northern Counties Paladin bus was new in 1993. Number 651 (K125 BUD) is seen on Oxford high street in December 1997. The bus was later transferred within the Go Ahead Group to Blue Star (Southampton), then Southern Vectis on the Isle of Wight. It still exists, partially converted to open-top.

Oxford Bus Company's number 41 (M627 FNS) is caught turning out of High Street in autumn 2000. New to Park's of Hamilton, near Glasgow, this Volvo B10M-60 has Belgian-built Jonckheere coachwork. It is being used on the X90 London service.

Another product of Volvo, a 1995-built B10B-58, is shown here in Oxford city centre in mid-1996. Number 602 (N602 FJO) carries Plaxton Verde B49F bodywork and is lettered for Oxford Bus Company's 'Cityline' services. The bus was later transferred to the Go Ahead Group's Dorset operations.

By autumn 2000, when this photo was taken, the low-floor double-decker had arrived in Oxford. Fleet number 110 (T110 DBW), adorned in park and ride green livery, is a 1999-built Dennis Trident, bodied by Alexander. It is seen crossing the Folly Bridge over the River Thames, on St Aldate's.

It is 22 May 2008 and Volvo B10B/Plaxton Verde 641 (P641 FFC) looks smart in Oxford Bus Company's latest red colour scheme. It is seen entering Oxford city centre, on local route 8. This bus was later sold to Dew's Coaches, Somersham, Cambridgeshire, where it was joined by several others on local bus routes.

The Oxford Bus Company has favoured Mercedes buses over the last few years. The first delivered for Oxford park and ride duties was 822 (MA52 OXF), a Citaro 0530. It is seen about to enter Broad Street in the city centre, 22 May 2008.

The similar Mercedes Citaro number 846 (HF55 OXF) received Oxford Bus Company's red livery. Here it is, on 20 May 2014, in the western outskirts of Didcot, operating a Thames Travel service to Wantage. Thames Travel had been purchased by the Go Ahead Group in 2011 and put under the same management.

Volvo supplied some of Oxford Bus Company's low-floor single-deck buses. Number 802 (T802 CBW) is one such. This B10BLE/Wright dual-doored saloon is seen in the latest paintwork at Oxford railway station, 22 May 2008 again.

Two Oxford Bus Company Volvo B10BLE/Wright saloons received historic liveries and I managed to photograph the pair on 22 May 2008. Number 816 (W816 FBW), delivered in 2000, looks beautiful in the old pre-NBC City of Oxford colours in Queen Street, Oxford.

Sister bus 817 (W817 FBW) received a version of Oxford Tramways Company livery, to celebrate 125 years of public transport in the city, in 2006. It is captured on St Aldate's in the city centre.

Do not be fooled by the 'cherished' registration of Oxford Bus Company's 361 (R11 OXF). It was new to the streets of Oxford in early 2013. This Wright Eclipse Gemini-bodied Volvo hybrid 'decker is seen near the railway station, heading for Blackbird Leys, on 20 May 2014.

Demonstrator SN59 AWW was on loan to Oxford Bus Company when I found it at the city's railway station on 20 May 2014. Given fleet number 900, this smart Alexander Dennis Enviro double-decker was being used on local route 5. The railway station now has its own bus terminal and many services use it today, as Gloucester Green is unable to accommodate many local routes.

Well-appointed modern coaches are used on the Oxford Bus Company's London express services, where they compete with Stagecoach, both operating to a high frequency. Soon to arrive at its Victoria terminus in the capital is number 81 (KF61 OXF), a Scania K360EB of 2011 delivery. It has a Plaxton Panther coach body, fitted with forty-four seats and a toilet. I photographed it on 23 January 2015.

The formation of South Midland coincided with the beginning of the widespread use of minibuses, such as this Ford Transit. Fleet number SM7 (B107 XJO) had a Dormobile bodyshell, finished off by Carlyle. It is seen in Gloucester Green, Oxford, in the spring of 1985.

South Midland's newly applied liveries and labelling are seen applied to Bicester depot and two of its inhabitants on 30 November 1985. On the left is ex-Potteries Motor Traction URF 51S, given the fleet number 51 by South Midland. This coach is a 1977-built Leyland Leopard/Duple Dominant. On the right is standard Bristol VR/ECW 466 (CJO 466R), inherited from Oxford South Midland. Photograph courtesy of Richard Huggins.

30 November 1985 was a dreary wet day, but Richard Huggins braved the poor weather to take some photographs of various South Midland depots. In the yard at Chipping Norton he found coach number 54 (EYH 808V). This Duple-bodied Leyland Leopard had been new to Grey Green of North London in 1980.

On the same date and at the same location as the previous photo, another Leyland Leopard/Duple Dominant coach combination is seen. This time it is number 17 (YFC 17V), new to Oxford South Midland, to whom it had been delivered in September 1979, seating forty-nine passengers.

An unusual minibus in the South Midland fleet was number 32 (D232 TBW), seen negotiating Carfax crossroads in Oxford city centre, summer 1987. Almost brand new at the time, this twenty-five-seat Optare City Pacer was built on a Volkswagen LT55 frame. Behind is an Oxford Bus Company Daimler Fleetline/Northern Counties 'decker, bought from Southend Transport.

Back to that dire day, 30 November 1985, and Richard Huggins has reached Witney depot. Here he found South Midland 32 (VUD 32X), a 1982-built Leyland Leopard with forty-nine-seat ECW coachwork. It is painted in the latest 'Orbiter' colour scheme, as were many other vehicles in the fleet. Alongside is sister coach 29 (VUD 29X), but this bears the earlier livery.

Richard Huggins also photographed South Midland 98 (EWW 204T) at Witney depot yard on that occasion. This Plaxton-bodied Leyland Leopard coach had been new in 1979 to Yorkshire coaching company Wallace Arnold, but used on their Devon touring operations. After use by South Midland, it was exported to Ireland, where it lasted until 2002.

Oxford South Midland bought fleet number 101 (EBW 101Y) new in April 1983. This Leyland Tiger/Duple Dominant coach was later transferred to South Midland, where it gained fleet number 125. It is seen, in the latest livery style of the time, at Gloucester Green, Oxford, in December 1986.

Demonstrating the rather overcomplicated South Midland 'Orbiter' livery is number 451 (TBW 451P), a Bristol VRT/SL3/6LX with ECW H43/31F, new to Oxford South Midland in June 1976. It is seen through the lens of Richard Huggins, in central Carterton, 30 November 1985.

This South Midland coach was originally registered A228 TMA when new to Martin of Middlewich, Cheshire, in 1983. Subsequent re-registrations saw it become 712 GRM, then A662 XDM (when with Stewart of Dalmuir, near Glasgow). Sold to South Midland in 1986, it is seen here at Gloucester Green, Oxford, in that year. Now numbered 127 (YYF 307), it is a Volvo B10M coach with Plaxton coachwork.

With the purchase of South Midland by Harry Blundred, of Devon General fame, the company was renamed Thames Transit. Fortunately, a more sober livery was adopted, as was the much greater use of minibuses. A typical example is 353 (G843 UDV), a 1990-built Mercedes 709D with twenty-nine-seat Carlyle bodywork. It is seen in Cornmarket Street (since pedestrianised), Oxford, in mid-1994.

Thames Transit brought something new to the British bus scene – the dual-doored minibus! Number 2006 (K707 UTT) is an Iveco 59.12. The bodybuilder, Mellor Coachcraft, had managed to cram in twenty-six seats. It is seen here by the Carfax Tower, in central Oxford, in early 1993, when the vehicle was almost new.

A larger bus in the Thames Transit fleet was number 996 (F279 HOD). This Leyland Tiger, with Plaxton bus bodywork, was new to Brixham Coaches, a firm taken over by Devon General. It was then transferred to Oxford, where it is seen, in Cornmarket Street, in mid-1994. This vehicle later saw further service with Tillingbourne, in Surrey.

Another transfer from Devon General was that of number 94 (LFJ 848W), a Bristol LH6L, built in 1980. The thirty-five-seat bodywork was a standard product of Eastern Coach Works. Lettered as a minibus, it is seen in central Oxford, on park and ride duties, on a sunny day in autumn 1989.

Thames Transit adopted the name 'Oxford Tube' for their frequent Oxford to London express services. This name is seen applied to Ikarus-bodied Volvo B10M coach number 24 (J499 MOD). It was photographed at the newly rebuilt Gloucester Green coach station, Oxford, in summer 1992.

Thames Transit number 6 (B403 UOD) was delivered new to Devon General, but was soon transferred to Oxfordshire for Oxford Tube duties. This Leyland Tiger/Duple Laser forty-four-seat coach is seen in central Oxford in the summer of 1987.

Also seen in Oxford's city centre in summer 1987 is Thames Transit number 9 (D142 PTT). Almost new at the time, this Leyland Tiger carries Plaxton Paramount III coachwork. The vehicle is picking up for London, the advertised day-return fare being £2.97.

George Street, in Oxford's city centre, is the location of this photograph taken in mid-1994. The bus is Thames Transit 3010 (L718 JUD), a Dennis Dart, new at the time. Bodywork, with dual doorway, is by Plaxton. It is painted in a special livery for the 'Blackbird Flyer' service working to and from the Blackbird Leys estate, which achieved notoriety in September 1991 after a spate of car thefts, followed by police action that resulted in riotous scenes.

Almost new Dennis Dart/Plaxton B37D number 3063 (R63UFC) is seen in a later version of the Blackbird Flyer livery. I photographed it in George Street, central Oxford, in late 1997. The bus later became Stagecoach number 23163.

Loading up at the Carfax crossroads in central Oxford is a most unusual bus, the only one of its type ever built. J227 OKX is the unique Iveco Turbo City 100 demonstrator, with Alexander R-type bodywork. The unusual front of the bus is due to the cowl being delivered as part of the chassis (as Mercedes have done for years). The Turbo City 100 was not a success, resulting in no orders, while J227 OKX was sold, later running for Filers of Devon and Bluebird of Greater Manchester. It is seen in early 1993, on loan to Thames Transit, on route 1 to Blackbird Leys.

New in 1996 as Thames Transit 3054, this Dennis Dart with single-door Plaxton Pointer bodywork is seen as Stagecoach Oxford number 754 (N54 KBW). I photographed it in Park End Street, in the west end of Oxford city centre, in autumn 2000. The bus later saw further service with Pennine Motor Service of Gargrave, Yorkshire.

A sister vehicle to the one featured in the last photo is seen in a much more rural location. Stagecoach Oxford 753 (N53 KBW) is passing the excellent Lamb Inn in West Hanney, a freehouse north of Wantage, in autumn 2000.

Another Stagecoach Oxford Dennis Dart is seen here, at Oxford railway station, in autumn 2000. Number 726 (P626 PGR) has an Alexander Dash single-door body. By the time of this photo, the railway station had become the terminus of many Oxford bus routes, as Gloucester Green was mainly reserved for coaches.

By autumn 2000 the low-floor bus had appeared on the streets of Oxford. In a modified version of Stagecoach Oxford's stripes, number 927 (S927 CFC), a MAN 18.220 of 1998 vintage, is seen between duties at St Giles, Oxford. It carries forty-two-seat Alexander bodywork. The bus was later transferred within the Stagecoach Group to Yorkshire.

After taking over Thames Transit, Stagecoach sensibly retained the Oxford Tube brand. The red livery is seen applied to W66 BBW, Stagecoach Oxford fleet number 66. This MAN 24.350LF, with a Jonckheere Monaco double-deck coach body, is seen leaving Oxford's High Street in autumn 2000. This vehicle later saw service in the Sheffield area with TM Travel.

From January 2003, Stagecoach brought all their fleets into one national five-figure numbering scheme. 22947 (OV51 KAK) loads up in Queen Street, beside the Carfax Tower, central Oxford, on 18 May 2008. Previously numbered 947, it is a MAN 18.220/Alexander B42F.

On the same occasion as the previous picture, again at the Carfax, Stagecoach 18052 (KX53 VNC) is seen in a special livery for the Oxford Brookes University service. Built by Transbus, the successor to Dennis at the time, this Trident has Plaxton bodywork. The Brookes Bus contract has since passed to the Oxford Bus Company. Meanwhile, 18052 has gone north to Stagecoach East Midlands.

On 18 May 2008, Stagecoach 15437 (KX08 KZE) was only a couple of months old when I photographed it in George Street, Oxford. Looking smart in Stagecoach's corporate livery, this is a Scania N230UD with Alexander Dennis bodywork to the Enviro standard.

Heading for its Gloucester Green terminus, passing the Carfax on 18 May 2008, Stagecoach 50120 (KP04 GKN) is operating an Oxford Tube service from London. This Neoplan Skyliner integral coach was later sold to an independent operator in Kent.

The Neoplans of Stagecoach were replaced by Van Hool TD92 integral eighty-seven-seat double-deck coaches for Oxford Tube services. One of these, number 50214 (OU09 FNH), is seen at its London terminus, with a sister coach behind, on Buckingham Palace Road, Victoria SW1, on the last day of May 2012.

In the mid-1970s, the dominant bus operator in Banbury was Midland Red. Prior to privatisation, this large company was split into four, with the north Oxfordshire services allocated to Midland Red South. This business was later sold to the Stagecoach Group. Back in 1974, the Ford R192/Plaxton Derwent was the standard service bus in Banbury, and I photographed Midland Red 6327 (YHA 327J) in the town's bus station with its pre-NBC livery.

New in 1977, to National Travel (South West), this Leyland Leopard/Willowbrook Spacecar coach was later purchased by Midland Red South for the X59 Banbury–Oxford service and similar duties. Number 67 (SAD 130R) is seen at Banbury bus station, laying over with two Iveco minibuses, in mid-1987.

Until rebuilding into a much smaller affair, Banbury bus station was situated beside the Oxford Canal, which connected the Thames at Oxford with the Grand Union system and the West Midlands. A narrowboat can be seen in the background as Midland Red South 1013 (PHH 613R) enjoys a rest here in the spring of 1993. This Duple Dominant coach-bodied Leyland Leopard was new as Cumberland Motor Services number 613 in 1977. Note that the fleetname of the company had reverted to Midland Red at the time.

Like many operators, Midland Red South had a phase of minibus operations. Number 451 (D451 CKV), a 1986-built Freight Rover Sherpa, is seen in Banbury bus station in mid-1987. Behind it is Leyland National 426, the only picture of this type of bus within these pages.

Number 371 (C729JJO), a Ford Transit twenty-seater, was an unusual minibus in the Midland Red South fleet. This vehicle had previously been in the Oxford South Midland fleet and is seen in Banbury bus station in spring 1993.

A more typical minibus with Midland Red South was number 882 (D882 CKV), an Iveco 49.10 with Robin Hood nineteen-seat dual-purpose bodywork. Delivered in December 1986, it is seen in Banbury bus station when around six months old.

Tanners Coaches of Banbury was a long-established company, with some rural stage carriage services. After deregulation in 1986, Tanners began operating some competitive town routes in Banbury. Unsurprisingly, this did not come as good news to the major operator in the area, Midland Red South. In 1990, therefore, Tanners sold out to the larger concern. In late 1990, a visit to Midland Red South's Banbury depot found two former Tanners coaches waiting to be photographed. Both are seen retaining their former liveries, but with Midland Red South fleet numbers. On the left is 1004 (RAA 873M), a Bedford YRT/Duple Dominant coach, new to Glider and Blue of Hampshire. To its right is 1007 (KIB 8140), a re-registered Leyland Leopard, again with Duple coachwork.

The use of 'cherished' registrations makes life very difficult when trying to trace the history of a particular bus or coach. It has proved impossible to discover anything about this Tanners coach, other than the obvious. MCH 189 is a DAF/Plaxton Supreme coach, seen here at the bus station in mid-1987, operating a Banbury town service.

Midland Red South was later taken over by the Stagecoach Group and the company's striped colour scheme was soon applied to the fleet. Fleet number 42586 (T586 SKG) is seen in Banbury in March 2003, carrying the corporate livery. This Mercedes Benz 0814D/ Plaxton minibus was new to Phil Anslow Travel of south Wales, another company that Stagecoach bought out. After use in the Oxfordshire area, this bus saw further use with Lloyds of Machynlleth, another Welsh operator.

Banbury's bus station was reduced in size sometime around the turn of the century, so many bus services were obliged to use the town centre streets. Stagecoach 34471 (KV53 NHF), a 2004-built Transbus Dart/Plaxton saloon, is seen near the market place on a local route on 29 June 2012.

Other Midland Red companies ran long-distance services into Oxfordshire. At Gloucester Green, Oxford, Midland Red West number 674 (SOA 674S) is awaiting its return journey to Worcester in the spring of 1985. This Leyland Leopard, built in 1978, carries Plaxton coachwork, one of many such vehicles distributed throughout the Midland Red empire. Midland Red West was later to be bought by First Group.

The Bristol Omnibus Company ran a regular Oxford–Swindon service using dual-purpose vehicles, such as 1966-built Bristol RELH6L/ECW 2043 (KHW 312E). This particular body style is one of the author's favourites. It is seen in Gloucester Green bus station, Oxford, *c*. 1975.

Like Midland Red, the Bristol Omnibus Company was split into various subsidiaries prior to privatisation of the NBC. Cotswold fleetnames are seen applied to the latest livery carried by 2087 (BHW 84J), photographed in Gloucester Green, Oxford, in January 1985. This 1971 Leyland Leopard, with Plaxton Elite forty-seven-seat coach body, was new as Bristol Omnibus Company number 2159.

A small part of southern Oxfordshire, around the Henley-on-Thames area, was formerly the territory of the Thames Valley Omnibus Company. During early NBC days, Thames Valley was combined with Aldershot & District to form Alder Valley. The Thatcher era saw the company split up again, prior to privatisation. Alder Valley North traded under the Bee-Line name, with Busy Bee fleetnames being applied to minibuses. Ford Transit minibus 326 (D826 UTF) carries this livery in Henley in the spring of 1987.

Arriva buses are a common sight in Oxford, running into the city from Aylesbury via Thame. The company also ran the Easybus network in and around Banbury. On such duties is Optare Solo number 0449 (Y49 HBT), seen in Banbury's rebuilt bus station in March 2003. This bus later saw operation in Plymouth with Target Travel.

Turning left from Oxford's high street in autumn 2000 is Arriva 539 (S159 KNK), approaching journey's end on the 280 from Aylesbury. This Volvo Olympian with Northern Counties bodywork, fitted with coach seats, was new in August 1998.

At the time of writing, early 2015, new buses are expected on Arriva's 280 route, which will oust buses such as this Sapphire-branded Alexander Dennis Enviro 400 'decker to other duties. Number 5440 (SN58 EOO) is seen at its Oxford terminating point, outside the railway station, on 20 May 2014.

The famous Warwickshire town of Stratford-upon-Avon was, until 1971, the home of a Midland Red subsidiary named Stratford Blue. By early 2000, when this photo was taken, the name had re-appeared on the scene, though only for a short period. The fleetname, if not the blue colours, is seen on S719 KNV, a Marshall-bodied Dennis Dart SLF found in Banbury on a rural service. The bus later saw service with Speedwell Travel of Derbyshire and Cavalier Travel in East Anglia.

The small Oxfordshire town of Didcot is known for its railway facilities and power station. It is also the home of Tappins Coaches. This long-established company undertakes various contracts, the occasional stage carriage work, private hire and tours. A visit to the small depot, sometime around 1974, found two vehicles sheltering out of the elements. On the left is Bedford VAM/Plaxton coach HJB 873D, while alongside is VTX 433, an ex-Rhondda Transport AEC Regent V/Weymann double-decker. The latter vehicle saw further life on driver training duties with Andrews of Sheffield.

A visit to Tappins Coaches in spring 1993 found a row of vehicles in the company's yard. Closest to the camera is YUE 338, a Volvo B10M-61 with Plaxton Paramount coachwork. New to Tappins in 1986, this vehicle was originally registered C326 UFP. Alongside is former London Transport DMS-type Fleetline OJD 401R, used on contract duties. On the far left we see open-top Leyland Atlantean/Alexander BFS 45L, owned by Lothian Regional Transport of Edinburgh, but used on Oxford sightseeing tours.

The Setright ticket machine beside the driver's position reveals that this vehicle was used on stage carriage duties. Tappins of Didcot 742 XMV is seen having a layover near St Giles in central Oxford in December 1986. This Leyland Leopard/Plaxton Supreme was new to National Travel South West in 1978, originally registered WFH 177S.

Edinburgh's Lothian Regional Transport operated city tours of Oxford during the 1990s and 2000s as a response to another operator running similar routes in the Scottish capital. As we have already seen, these used Tappins' Didcot depot as an operating base. In the late 1990s, BFS 34L, named the *Oxford Graduate*, is seen awaiting customers at Oxford railway station. The vehicle is a Leyland Atlantean AN68/1R with open-top Alexander bodywork, new with a roof as number 34 in 1973.

Lothian Regional Transport later replaced its Atlanteans with Alexander-bodied, open-top Leyland Olympians. Originally numbered 300 in the parent fleet, it was delivered to Edinburgh with a roof in 1988. E300 MSG is seen in Oxford city centre during autumn 2000. This bus later went to Sanders of Holt, Norfolk, for further tourist service.

Tourists were well provided for in Oxford during the early years of the twenty-first century. The Oxford Full Circle Tour competed with other operators for the sightseeing trade. On a rainy day in May 2004, customers are in short supply in central Oxford as ex-West Midlands PTE MCW Metrobus Mark II NOA 451X loads up. Not a day for open-top operation!

The City Sightseeing operations are seen in many cities worldwide, including Oxford. In these colours at Oxford railway station in summer 2004 is GJZ 9574. Originally registered STK 124T, this is an ex-Plymouth City Transport Leyland Atlantean AN68/1R with Roe bodywork converted to open-top. A Leyland Olympian stands behind.

A former Dublin Bus Leyland Olympian/Alexander is seen just off Broad Street in Oxford city centre, on 22 May 2008. MUI 7853, painted in City Sightseeing's colours, was new as 90-D-1012. This bus was later exported to Zimbabwe.

Chiltern Queens, an independent based in the south Oxfordshire village of Woodcote, ran several services in the Didcot, Wallingford and Reading areas. Seen in front of Wallingford's war memorial *c.* 1975 is LMO 745, a 1955-built AEC Reliance with Duple (Midland) forty-four-seat bodywork. This vehicle was new to Chiltern Queens.

At Chiltern Queens depot *c.* 1975 is YNX 478, an AEC Reliance new to Black & White of Harvington, Worcestershire, in 1958. Chiltern Queens had removed the original body and replaced it with one from 530 BPG, built by Duple (Midland).

Seen when almost new, in 1974, is Chiltern Queens OJO 835M, photographed in front of the Corn Exchange in Wallingford. Most of the company's buses at the time were built by AEC, so this particular bus, a Leyland Leopard, was quite unusual. Plaxton Derwent bodywork features.

Though Chiltern Queens buses carried red livery, the company's coach fleet was smartly turned out in two-tone green. This is seen applied to 135 KD, a 1962 AEC Reliance with Burlingham coachwork. This coach was new to Watercroft of Bradford. My late friend Les Flint took this photo for me at the depot yard in June 1981.

Worth's Coaches, based at Enstone in north Oxfordshire, is a long-established bus and coach operator still in business today. Here is one of their service buses at Gloucester Green, Oxford, in 1974, ready to return to its home village. NPM 326F is a Ford R192 with Strachans forty-five-seat dual-purpose bodywork, new to Woburn of London WC1.

A visit to the Worth's depot yard in April 2005 found some modern vehicles on display. BU53 ZWZ, a 2004-built Mercedes O530 Citaro forty-two-seater, bought new, is on the left. This bus was later sold to Western Greyhound in Cornwall. Alongside is BBW 216Y, a 1982 Leyland Olympian/ECW, new to Oxford South Midland.

A rare vehicle in the fleet of Worth's of Enstone was GNF 7V, one of a small batch of Park Royal bodied Leyland Titans purchased by Greater Manchester Transport in 1979. It is seen in Worth's depot yard in March 1993, accompanied by JWL 322W, one of three Volvo B58 coaches bought new in 1982.

One of my favourite Oxfordshire independent operators has long been Charlton-on-Otmoor Services, based in the village of the same name, about 4 miles south of Bicester. The business is still trading, though few stage carriage duties are now undertaken. Back in the 1970s, though, their buses could regularly be seen in Oxford. At the depot in 1974, I found 988 VRR, an ex-Barton of Nottinghamshire 1964-built AEC Reliance/Harrington coach. This was used regularly on the service to Oxford. Behind are two ex-London Transport AEC RT types, HLX 215 (out of use) and KGU 239.

Here is 988 VRR again, seen in the 'local coaches' boarding area at Gloucester Green, Oxford, being ignored by a fellow bus enthusiast, who was more interested in the Oxford South Midland offerings behind. Though I have no exact date, this would have been *c.* 1975.

Charlton-on-Otmoor Services-owned 719 FHA is seen on bus duty in Cornmarket Street, Oxford, in 1974. This Leyland Tiger Cub PSUC1/2 with Harrington C41F coachwork was new to Gliderways of Smethwick, Birmingham, in 1958. Apart from preserved vehicles, this is the last coach I saw with a tailfin, a common sight in the 1950s. Cornmarket Street has since been pedestrianised.

At Gloucester Green, Oxford, in 1980, we see Charlton-on-Otmoor Services 456 KTG. This 1961-built AEC Regent V/Metro-Cammell double-decker was new to Rhondda Transport of South Wales, but became a stalwart on the Oxford route.

Not all Charlton-on-Otmoor Services vehicles were second-hand. Here is GUD 708L, a 1972-built Leyland Leopard/Plaxton Elite Express fifty-one-seater bought new. It is seen at Gloucester Green, Oxford, in 1981 on stage carriage duties.

Geoff Amos Coaches of Daventry, Northamptonshire, ran bus services into Banbury until the company went out of business in 2011. Back in 1974, I found FRY 708D at Banbury's bus station. This 1966 Bedford VAM 5/Strachans B50F service bus was new to another Northamptonshire business, Owens of Upper Boddington.

Staying at Banbury bus station, but in mid-1987, we see TVV 170W in the Geoff Amos fleet. This bus, bought new by the company in 1980, is a Bedford YMT with Duple Dominant bodywork, seating fifty-three.

The last two decades of the twentieth century saw Geoff Amos Coaches purchasing some rather unusual buses for the stage carriage routes. XAM 731A was a rare Dennis Dorchester with a Wadham Stringer bus body, bought new. It is seen at Banbury bus station in mid-1987.

B368 KNH was another Dennis Dorchester in the Geoff Amos fleet, this time with Reeve Burgess bodywork. It later saw service with Stuarts of Carluke, Scotland, but is seen here in Banbury bus station in the spring of 1994.

On a market day in March 2003 we see Geoff Amos Coaches YC51 HAO, just arrived in Banbury from over the Northamptonshire border. This thirty-three-seat Optare Solo was bought new in 2001. It was eventually sold to E. & M. Horsburgh, a Scottish bus company in the Livingston area.

Heyfordian Coaches, based at the village of Upper Heyford, have been trading since the 1940s. The firm's activities today include several stage carriage services, school runs and various contracts, using a fleet of over seventy vehicles. A visit to the depot in 1977 found two unusual buses laying over between duties. On the left is NAL 545F, an ex-West Bridgeford UDC AEC Swift/East Lancs, while the other bus is NJW 716E, a rare Daimler Roadliner with Strachans bodywork, new to Wolverhampton Corporation.

Photographed outside Heyfordian's yard in 1981 is FWY 198C. Somewhat rebuilt around the front end, this Leyland Leopard/Duple Commander coach was used mainly on schools duties. It was new to W. R. & P. Bingley of West Yorkshire, who often used it on United Services stage carriage routes.

On the last day of November 1985, Richard Huggins found this Heyfordian coach parked at Cuckold's Holt Farm near Gagingwell, Oxfordshire. BNO 695T is a 1979-built Bedford YMT with Duple Dominant coachwork. Note the folding bus-type doors, a feature of many similar coaches, enabling the vehicle to be used on stage services and attracting a government grant at the time. This particular coach was new to Eastern National.

Heyfordian's OBW 399M, a Seddon Pennine 6/Willowbrook coach seating fifty-one passengers, is seen in Gloucester Green, Oxford, awaiting departure time *c.* 1976. New to Hambridge of Kidlington, this vehicle remained in the Oxford area and later saw service with Motts of Upton, in whose hands I photographed it in 1980 – see it again on page 87.

Heyfordian also undertake high-class touring work and a fleet of very smart coaches is maintained for these duties. In 1981, parked at the depot, is XWL 804R, an AEC Reliance/ Plaxton Supreme coach fitted with an air conditioning unit. Heyfordian purchased this vehicle new in 1977.

The Plaxton Primo integral midibus was not a popular vehicle with many operators, but Heyfordian purchased KX58 LJC for stage carriage work. It is seen here near Banbury's market place on 29 June 2012.

On the corner of Magdalen Street and Broad Street, central Oxford, Heyfordian's twenty-nine-seat Optare Solo YJ59 NNM waits for passengers on route 25A to Bicester on 13 December 2011. This service has since passed to Thames Travel.

The Optare Solo is a popular vehicle for rural Oxfordshire bus services. Here is W83 NDW, owned by Z&S of Aylesbury, in Thame town centre departing for Brill. This twenty-seat bus was new to Bebb's Coaches of Llantwit Fadre, South Wales. Thame's Christmas lights are up and ready for use, as the date is 14 December 2011.

Windrush Valley Coaches once ran a rural service into Woodstock, a small Oxfordshire town famous for Blenheim Palace. In the summer of 1990, F480 AKC, a Mercedes 609D coach-seated minibus, was found in the town centre on arrival.

For a short time in the 1990s, a firm called Oxon Travel ran competitive bus services between Oxford and Bicester, using a variety of smaller vehicles. On such duties in Bicester during mid-1994 is ATH 108T, a Bristol LHS6L with Plaxton coachwork. Originally registered FTW 133T, it was new to Essex operator Harris Coaches of Grays.

At Bicester's tiny bus station, again in mid-1994, is Oxon Travel KJD 431P. Still in London Transport red, this is a 1976-built Bristol LH6L with thirty-nine-seat ECW bodywork, numbered BL31 when in London service.

Seddon Pennine 6/Willowbrook OBW 399M is seen again at Gloucester Green, Oxford, this time in early 1980, in the hands of a Buckinghamshire-based company, Motts of Upton. The business later moved to Aylesbury and, after deregulation, greatly expanded the stage carriage work undertaken.

Using the alternative name of 'Yellow Bus', Motts of Aylesbury-owned JHE 143W arrives in Oxford in early 1993, passing one of the city's 'dreaming spires' on High Street. New to South Yorkshire PTE as number 1843, it is an MCW Metrobus Mark 1 delivered in 1981.

House's Coaches, based in the small Oxfordshire town of Watlington, ran a few rural stage carriage routes, including one to Wallingford, as can be seen on the destination display. WXC 343 is seen at the depot in 1977. New to Orange Luxury Coaches of London, it is a 1959-built Bedford SB8 with thirty-seven-seat Harrington Crusader coachwork.

A nice rural occasion at Broughton, west of Banbury, on 12 July 1974. 641 TPG of Mathews Coaches has just deposited a couple of passengers and will soon depart towards Brailes. No doubt the ladies will have retained their Bellgraphic tickets, for each one had a prayer printed on the reverse side – a nice touch. The coach is a Bedford SB8 of 1961, with forty-one-seat Duple bodywork. It was bought new by Whites Coaches of Camberley.

Thames Travel was a newcomer to the Oxfordshire bus scene in the last years of the twentieth century. The company expanded rapidly throughout the south of the county and into Berkshire. A smart blue and green livery was applied to the fleet, but number 451 (KP51 UFG) has not yet received it as it approaches the Carfax along St Aldate's in Oxford's city centre. Photographed in the summer of 2004, it is a low-floor Plaxton-bodied Dennis Dart, new to Thames Travel in 2002. Prominent in the background is the famous Old Tom bell tower.

Thames Travel's full livery is displayed on number 205 (AE05 EUZ) as it passes along New Road in Oxford city centre, heading towards the railway station on 22 May 2008. This bus is a MAN 14.220 with MCV Evolution forty-seat body. Thames Travel became part of the Go Ahead Group in 2011, but to date has been retained as a separate entity.

RH Transport made the local headlines when it abruptly ceased trading in October 2012. Prior to that, the company had run several bus services in and around Oxfordshire. Optare Solo MX55 WDJ is seen on such duties in central Oxford on 22 May 2008.

Courtney Buses mainly operate in Berkshire, but have recently gained a contract in Oxfordshire, running the Milton Park Shuttle in Didcot. At that town's railway station on 20 May 2014 is SN63 VTZ, a smart Alexander Dennis Enviro 400 double-decker.

Banbury-based Cheney Travel ran some stage carriage services for a while. The company still exists, but confines its business to coaching activities. For the bus routes Cheney bought W3 CTS, a Caetano-bodied Dennis Dart SLF, seen here arriving in Banbury town centre in March 2003. This vehicle later passed to Milton Keynes City Bus, then on into the main Arriva fleet.

The village of Wheatley, between Thame and Oxford, was once home to Plastow's Coaches, with a rather interesting collection of vehicles used mainly on schools and contract duties. Sometime around 1975, I visited the depot and found this fine coach waiting to be photographed. 8750 HA was a Bedford VAL14/Harrington (not a common combination) new to West Midlands operator Morris of Bearwood.

Another Plastow's vehicle was HMO 852, an ex-Thames Valley Bristol LS6G/ECW forty-five-seater, seen awaiting another schools duty at the depot, *c.* 1975. The Commer towing vehicle alongside is also of note.

Very close to the Oxford South Midland depot in Wantage were the premises of Regent Coaches. On 22 April 1974, a pair of beautiful Bedfords was to be found in the yard. To the left is PUJ 789, an SB3/Duple, while to its right is similar SUJ 126. The latter had been new to Salopia of Whitchurch, Shropshire.

Premier Travel of Cambridge, jointly with Percivals of Oxford, ran an express service between the two university cities. This ran via Luton and Hitchin, rather than Milton Keynes, Bedford and St Neots as on today's Stagecoach X5. Back in 1974, fleet number 235 (DWD 194C) is seen at Gloucester Green, Oxford, prior to returning to its home city. This 1965 AEC Reliance/Harrington coach, one of many in the fleet, was originally new to Bermuda of Nuneaton.

Many National Express long-distance services called at Oxford's Gloucester Green bus station, often for a refreshment stop. Crosville's CLL313 (RMA 313P) is seen outside the café, probably en route from Wales to London, when the coach was almost brand new. Delivered in 1976, it is a Plaxton-bodied Leyland Leopard.

Also seen at Gloucester Green, *c.* 1975, is Eastern Scottish YH524A (BSG 524L), a 1973 Leyland Leopard with the famous Alexander Y-type coachwork. It is presumed to be returning to the bus station to pick up its passengers, prior to onward travel to London.

National Express also served Banbury bus station. Here, in 1974, among the Midland Red service buses, is Standerwick 52 (LRN 52J), a 1971 Bristol VRL/ECW double-deck coach, no doubt on a journey from the North West to London. Standerwick was then the name of the coaching arm of Ribble Motor Services, but the name was to disappear shortly after the photo was taken.

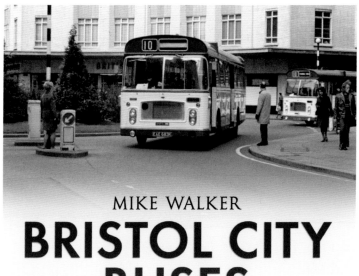

Also available from Amberley Publishing

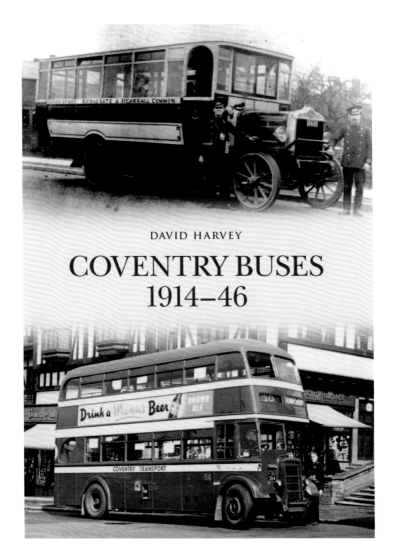

DAVID HARVEY

COVENTRY BUSES
1914–46

Coventry Buses 1914-46
David Harvey

David Harvey examines the Coventry bus fleet from when it first
began in 1914 to 1946.

978 1 4456 4704 3

Available from all good bookshops or to order direct
Please call **01453-847-800**
www.amberley-books.com